OBSERVATIONS FROM THE WOUNDED YAK

A relationship's journey through space and time

By Joanne Mytts & David Coull

Tellwell Talent
www.tellwell.ca

ISBN
978-0-2288-0036-1 (Paperback)
978-0-2288-0037-8 (eBook)

OBSERVATIONS FROM THE WOUNDED YAK

TABLE OF CONTENTS

INTRODUCTION

As told by Holt the Yak...

The most considerate gift
you can give a loved one
is your undivided attention.
tpb

Hello. My name is Holt, and I am a yak. A wounded yak, to be precise. This book contains a series of thoughts and observations I have made about life, people, and relationships over a period of about twenty years, which happens to be most of my life. I've chosen one particular couple, David and Joanne, as my focus because I've observed them for quite some time now, and I have come to realize that they are a rather curious pair. I find them interesting because of how they seem to relate to, support, and grow with one another, all while living life to what seems to be the fullest these days. Besides, they didn't just fall off the yak-drawn turnip truck. They have some great insights and philosophies that I know both individuals and other couples will benefit from.

The book is formatted for you to think, react, and interact with what you are reading. At the bottom of each page is a small notes section where you can write any thoughts or questions you may have. The "something to chew on" at the end of each chapter has been designed to provide you with further ideas for thought, study, or self-reflection.

Before you begin reading, I thought it would be prudent for me to conduct an interview with the authors — David and Joanne. This will allow you, the reader, to have an idea of the reasons behind this book as well as the reasons why the book has been formatted in this way.

1. *Holt:* What prompted you to write this book?
   Joanne: David prompted me to write the book. He thought it would be a good idea as he was very supportive and encouraging with my tpb collection and suggested I put it into a book. From there, it was a short step to both of us collaborating in putting this book together. We decided to incorporate tpb into a larger book with a tpb per chapter.

2. *Holt:* I see that there's a "tpb" after each chapter title. What exactly is tpb?
   Joanne: Tpb is "the purple blanket". The purple blanket is a place where I sit and write down thoughts and observations. David encouraged me to write more tpbs and eventually publish them. The tpbs under each chapter title were chosen because they are the best fit for

_____

_____

_____

the content of that chapter. We still sit on tpb and chat, drink tea, and meditate. This special place in our home is, in fact, an actual blanket!

3. *Holt:* When did you start working on this book?
   Joanne: The book began in mid 2017.

4. *Holt:* How difficult was it to develop the ideas of the book?
   Joanne: The ideas and topics of the book came to us initially as a result of our own observations of ourselves, and of others. We began talking to people about our experiences. We found that many people were in similar or other difficult situations and did not know how to change. We thought a book of our observations may help people to look more closely at their own situations. Whether good or bad, there is always room for improvement.

5. *Holt:* Where was it written? Did the location have any bearing on the ease of writing?
   David: The book was written in the hills and valleys of Vancouver Island, coffee shops, the Canadian Rocky Mountains, a plane 12,000 metres over the Pacific Ocean, and in a small New Zealand town. It was a great experience no matter where we were writing. The feeling of being immersed in a natural landscape of forests, valleys, and mountains certainly helped the creative process.

6. *Holt:* Can you explain the great chapter titles to me?
   David and Joanne: Each chapter title arose from topics we had talked about. Each chapter title has a specific series of related observations.

_____

_____

_____

7. *Holt:* Yes, but how did you choose those *specific* words?

    David: Well, for example, Joanne turned to me one day and said, "You love me very well." Thus, the chapter title was born. You can love people, but you can also love them very well.

8. *Holt:* I see you have a somewhat eclectic set of references.

    David: Yes — we like to take information from a wide array of sources so as to provide a balanced perspective for our ideas. We used philosophical texts, economic and sociological references, as well as books from the Buddhist and Judaeo-Christian traditions.

9. *Holt:* Does the choice of these books reflect your backgrounds at all?

    David: Yes, I grew up in what could loosely be called a Judaeo-Christian milieu.

    Joanne: My interest in society and culture prompted me to study sociology. Spending a significant amount of time in Asia introduced me to the philosophies of Buddhism. By swapping thoughts and ideas, we found remarkable similarities between these backgrounds — far more than what could be attributed to chance alone.

THE CROW APPLAUDS

As told by Holt the Yak....

After all of the storms,
All of the unrest,
All of the noise,
They still shone for each other.
tpb

When we travel through life, our path is our own — as we travel along we are at the centre of our own stage. Travelling along our path provides us with a means to experience ourselves in a wide variety of situations. Our journey can provide intense experiences through which we are able to confront our fears, strengths, and weaknesses. It may also be that our opinions and attitudes to both ourselves and others may be challenged, changed, or both. We can think in new ways and absorb our new encounters in what can be a transformative experience. Our mental horizons will open for us. This can help us to develop a more self-reflective approach to life.

We will still take our own problems seriously, but we are able to put them into a wider context and see them in more relative terms.

When we are listening, really deeply listening, we are present in the moment. During this presence, we make no attempt to either control or judge what is being said. We simply need to listen to precisely what is being said.

Listening is not a passive activity and should not be treated as such. We should listen actively. If we are actively focused on what we are hearing, rather than planning our next statement, this will allow us to turn what we are hearing into meaning. We also need to be committed to our own self-control, as we are listening to understand rather than listening to simply respond. If we are truly listening to another person, we could consider the following qualities as being important: offering nonverbal feedback, being present in the moment, and being connected with whomever we are listening to.

We hear in equal measure to what we listen with. When we listen with our mind we understand more of life. We first hear words, both negative and positive words. Although we hear the words, we may not yet fully understand the words. An example may be, "You look beautiful today." We recognise the words as positive, but it takes time for the words, if we consider them, to be actually felt. When we listen with our heart we feel more of life. We begin to live and experience the words. When told we are beautiful, we feel beautiful. When we listen with both our being and our spirit, we are transformed and we are joined with life itself. We actually

_____

_____

_____

"live" the words. We become complete with our environment (people, nature, selves, situations, vibrations, etc.), reprogramming ourselves to believe.

We have listened to each other over a long period of time and space. From this, we have come to live and believe each other's words. This has allowed us to not only wholly experience what we hear, but to return it to the source should we choose to do so. This is one method by which we can completely love our partner. This is also how we listen to what is happening in our lives and how we can have a fully experiential relationship with ourselves.

If we are willing to listen at an intimate and complete level, with everything in our being, we may be fortunate enough to be touched by the encounter. We don't miss it, for it becomes a part of us. This can be an overwhelming, even painful experience, and/or it can be wonderfully fulfilling.

The work of being is an invitation into a deeper relationship with life. This can wait for us in the unfolding of events that occur in our daily lives. The opening of our eyes, breath, and heart enables us to partake in this relationship that we can have with life. Opportunities can exist everywhere and anywhere. All that we require is the awareness to see them for what they are. These opportunities wait for us in each breath and feeling. We must recognise a window of opportunity, realising that it may open from the other side at times, via another person. This very thing happened to Joanne, causing her to decide to depart from Korea. Joanne's recognition came about via another person who caused a life-changing incident. Even though Joanne had decided that she wanted to return to Canada, she

_____

_____

_____

couldn't see a reason for doing so. Perhaps no window had presented itself to her, or more likely she wasn't able to see any windows present. It wasn't until she'd had a very strenuous and difficult time involving another person that Joanne decided it was time to leave Korea and return to Canada. I suspect that other windows and experiences had to be ready for Joanne, and conversely Joanne had to be ready for them, in order for the timing to have been just right for her to finally make her decision. Finally, after realising the opportunity, we must not be too afraid to pass through the window, for the opportunity is often lost with time and hesitation. An example of this could be expressing your feelings for another. There will be no other time like that moment. The risk or uncertainty that is associated with opportunities will affect how we react to them. We can choose to either take action or not take action. In order to make the most of what is presented, we need to have confidence in ourselves to express our thoughts and feelings.

> *"There are moments which mark your life. Moments when you realise nothing will ever be the same and time is divided into two parts: before this and after this"*
>
> *Fallen*

Moments in our lives, such as these, may take us by surprise, or they may be planned for. Either way, their significance is just as great and has a huge impact on our lives. You may find that you are not just writing yourself a new chapter in your life, but a whole new story. If this inspiration arises

_____

_____

_____

from open and honest introspection and self-reflection and provides opportunities for growth, then the new story is well worth writing. A change for the better, no matter how difficult it may be to make, is always a change worth making and a chance worth taking.

Their choice to reunite upon Joanne's return from Korea blatantly marked a point in their relationship that was a new beginning. They both stepped into a space which was a 'now or never' moment, a space where they realised that they would take that moment to allow a new bud of their relationship to blossom. That was the moment from which these two souls would join and move forward together, although they weren't yet aware of this.

Every relationship has a beginning, a middle, and an end, although none of these places may be apparent. Alternatively, some of these places may be stark. Your relationship will have a solid foundation when it is based on mutual understanding, the will to understand, and happiness. If your relationship is instead based on fear or uncertainty, it assuredly will not have this grounding. The foundations of our relationships may be added onto by importing behaviours and beliefs from former relationships. This building process can be both beneficial and detrimental. We must be aware of our nurturing, loving words and behaviours, and we must apply them to our new, blossoming relationship. We must also be aware of our neglectful, damaging words and behaviours, and take time to reflect and replace the negativity with positive, nurturing love. Triggers (negative emotional responses) from former relationships may cause confusion and damage in our current relationships.

_____

_____

_____

We must remember that the behaviours we are witnessing are not from the people in our past. Even if the behaviour and words are the same, our response needn't be. For example, comparing an important person in our present with someone in our past is not meant as criticism but rather as a simple observation. We need to make an effort to know each other so we realise that we are not criticising.

If others are unwilling to accept us and our true nature, then no actions on our part are needed. Silently let them be themselves while we remain ourselves. If we cannot be loved in an unconditional manner, it is ineffectual to try to convince the other to accept us, for they are not there; they are not in the space or frame of mind they need to be in the relationship.

How can we know our true nature? Life presents us with an endless series of challenges, obstacles, and fortunes. When these events happen, we can act or react from our own essence. It is quite possible to meet an extraordinary situation with a very ordinary response. For example, you may have found yourself stopping to help at the scene of a bad car crash "because it was the right thing to do." In our daily life, there is ample material that we can use for the development of our true nature. We should not fall into the all-too-common trap of believing we are simply the sum of our worst traits. Our minds will naturally want to attain what is advantageous to us and to avoid that which is not. By using your heart and mind you can move beyond these often unworthy or unwarranted feelings and begin to experience a measure of freedom that comes with the realization that you're not the sum of your worst traits.

_____

_____

_____

Past events, be they traumatic or otherwise, no longer belong to you (see "the past is not my home" in a later chapter). Furthermore, these past events do not define your true nature. The intensity of your desires or fears (be they from the past or the present) may be used as a source of energy that will allow you to connect with what really matters. We often do not have a choice regarding what occurred in our personal history. However, we are free to choose those events from our past that will lead us to a deeper understanding of our true nature. True nature, according to Buddhist philosophy, may be an emptiness from which other states such as love, kindness, and compassion may arise.

> *"We shall not cease from our exploration, and at the end of our exploring will be to arrive where we started and know the place for the first time."*
>
> *T.S. Eliot*

It's most important to keep an open mind regarding ourselves and our situations, as there are always new perspectives and/or opportunities to be found. Our true nature arises when we realise what is present without qualities, the material qualities we seem to rely on.

> *"Dance with the love that moves the stars."*
>
> *Cynthia Bourgeault*

As our relationships grow and develop, we are more inclined to share the path and the experiences our relationships have to offer. Together we are able to absorb the lessons that life has for us. As we travel along life's path we are able to share and accumulate these experiences. The fact that the path has been trodden before allows us to see connections that occur over vast distances of both time and space. If we see and listen with our completeness, we can be aware of our paths intersecting and coming and going with others. Each and every one of these connections can be a learning opportunity for us to grow.

It is sometimes difficult to realise our situation until we decide to leave it. Once free of an abusive or toxic relationship, we may then begin to understand the effects by listening to and understanding similar stories shared by others.

As we were writing this book, we made a series of connections spanning two thousand years and half a world:

Two thousand years ago...
The path of Mary Magdalene, according to the Nag Hammadi Gospels: The path of conscious love comes in different versions. The path Mary Magdalene chose was to keep the heart clear and unencumbered.

One hundred years ago...
Robert Frost – "The Road Not Taken":
Different options were available and the path less travelled was the path taken.

_____

_____

_____

Twenty years ago...

John Welwood:

"Long term relationships can follow different paths;

To either awaken our true nature and promote and reflect who we are in a conscious relationship, or they can be function over feeling."

All three of these examples show that people are able to choose their own path. Despite these paths being widely separated in both time and space, they can still be similar. We are walking in the footsteps of those who have gone before, be they great, humble, or somewhere in between. These luminaries were all following a path, and in all probability, this path had been trodden before, irrespective of its place and time. However, people sometimes think that they are the first and only ones to have ever experienced a path. These people do not accept or realise that their path has been travelled before. As a result of their self-absorption, these people are oblivious to the timeless ebb and flow of life.

Conscious relationships consist of our efforts, awareness, desires, and sacrifices, whereas function over feeling means we choose to have a more functional relationship that serves a purpose, such as raising a family. This society in which we live consists of a number of "expectations" that require a relationship that is more suited for function. We are expected to complete high school and perhaps go on to university. Then, not much later, we are expected to find a job, meet a suitable partner, get married, buy a house, and start a family. All this time we are not having a conscious relationship with ourselves or our partner; instead, we are simply performing a "function".

_____

_____

_____

A conscious relationship is one in which both partners are committed to a specific sense of purpose, growth, or perhaps collective growth. When people come together with the intention of growing together (rather than coming together to simply meet their own individual needs, thereby allowing expectations to erode the relationship), then the relationship will tend to move toward the higher goal of that in which each person will support and encourage the other to develop and grow. Life is all about growth, be it mental, spiritual, or physical. If we are dedicated to experiencing growth, we will, almost by default, be dedicated to keeping a relationship both vibrant and alive. Growth, being inclined to move toward the unknown, can be frightening. However, approaching the unknown together will allow the relationship to remain solid and enriching. David and Joanne's relationship has always had an inclination to grow. Whether they've always been aware of the growth or not, they've later come to realise the significance of that growth.

Past troubles (from past relationships) can be triggered in a new relationship. When bad feelings arise, they are often accompanied by feelings of unease or alarm. We need to realise that these feelings are not caused by our partner, but by our own beliefs which have grown out of our past. If we recognise the source of our beliefs, then we can identify and face these beliefs. We can then (if necessary) break them down and develop new or changed beliefs. In this way the patterns or habits from our past will also be broken down.

_____

_____

_____

In the conscious relationship, the importance of honesty cannot be over-stated. If we feel safe and loved, we can share those parts of ourselves which may be difficult or unpleasant and we can let our partners do the same. This sharing will in turn allow us to feel known and understood.

Realizing the importance of allowing our partners to look after us or take care of us in a non-threatening manner is essential in a mutually nurturing relationship. In the past, I have observed both David and Joanne in situations where people have offered financial help to them. They have declined because they had little trust that this kind of help was free of future obligations. However, in a supportive relationship, there are no expectations of future payment, only of mutual support.

Our path may be ours alone or parallel with another's. Over time, our paths may converge or diverge. If, as is wont to happen, two formerly parallel paths converge, then a shared journey can begin. The wonder and magic of a shared journey is far greater than that experienced by an individual one. The love, sharing, obstacles, joys, and wonder are all part of the pageant that makes a shared life a treasure beyond compare. There are clear options to choose from as we travel along life's journey. If we choose the journey that provides us with the nurturing, love, safety, and wonder we desire, then the crows will most assuredly applaud!

I can confidently say that these two have no regrets. They have learned and grown from each and every experience that they have enjoyed and endured — everything from moving across continents, to gaining further education, to job choices. Perhaps when we feel regret, we have a perception of how things should have been. Therefore, if we change our perception of how things are in the present, then we may change whether or not we experience regret from the past.

In our immediate lives, there is a little of the past and a little of the future. The process of accepting the past can be difficult. Allow yourself to see the past for what it really was. Accepting the past, hard though this may be, can allow you to alter your perception of it so you can be free to live in the present moment. Live mindfully in the present. Be aware of your inner world (thoughts, emotions, and breath) and also of your outer world (your surroundings and your reactions to them). Observe your own thoughts while quieting the noise. Do not fear your future. Enjoy the present but let the future unfold. Right now, *in this moment,* you are who and where you need to be. Do not try to be (or wish you were) someone or somewhere else. In doing this, you are failing to live your life in the present moment, the only moment there is.

There is an empty space immediately ahead waiting for us to move into. It may be too close to notice easily, but it exists. We may fear stepping into the unknown, and the space may be transitory. It is difficult at times, but as we move forward we are able to grow and occupy the space while successive new spaces are continually being formed. These spaces may even be formed by ourselves as we require them.

_____

_____

_____

"I want to unfold

I don't want to stay folded anymore

Because where I am folded, I am out of touch with the truth."

Rilke

_____

_____

_____

SOMETHING TO CHEW ON...

1. Think of five "dots" in your past. These dots are events that may be seemingly unrelated. Now try to connect these dots. If you are able to connect them, consider how have they worked together to bring you to where you are presently on your life's journey.

2. Consider a window of opportunity that has presented itself to you. Think of what happened when you either a) moved forward with the opportunity, or b) failed to seize it. Did other opportunities subsequently present themselves?

3. How can behaviours from previous relationships affect your current relationship? What, if any, long-term effects may accrue from these imported behaviours?

4. In what way do you see yourself at the centre of your own life's stage? How do you respond to your position there?

_____

_____

_____

YOU LOVE ME VERY WELL

As told by Holt the Yak...

The soul finds its mate long before the mind is upon it.
It's the one whom you crave, not only when you are alone.
It's the one who seduces you without touch.
And the one with whom you find solace.
tpb

Sometimes we are in a loving relationship before we realise it. Is there such a thing as love at first sight? There is most certainly a draw or an attraction between people who are right for each other. Relationships of various lengths and depths come into and out of our lives, but the ones to whom our souls are drawn, the ones who cannot be avoided or denied, those are the ones who will make a lasting impression on us. A deep and enduring relationship, perhaps a lifelong companion, is often the result of such an experience, or, for want of a better phrase, "love at first sight". A slight change in our vibrations will cause a more pronounced change in our lives. Changing vibrations cause some to become attracted to us, and others to be repulsed.

When they met, the circumstances were such that they were able to get to know one another via a shared interest in martial arts. Upon meeting, David and Joanne were able to instantly recognise each other's vibrations. The mutual feeling was that of comfort, familiarity, and a desire to get to know the other more. Following their first meeting, they would look forward to and excitedly greet each other at their Aikido classes each week.

While building and continuing to build such a relationship, one experiences a warm comfort at the sight, thought, and touch of this special person. Once a conscious decision has been made to cultivate the relationship, the most important action for all involved is to share experiences. There is a point in a relationship where we decide we want to spend the rest of our life with a person. If fortunate enough to have this choice, we must leave the past and move forward in order to grow in our relationship.

At some points, Joanne and David were unable to see each other for periods of years. During these times, they did what was needed in order to maintain their relationship. They were able to cultivate their friendship via the modern expedient of email. For fifteen years, simple updates on daily goings on, plans and adventures, along with infrequent visits allowed them to remain friends.

Remaining friends is most important because only time spent together allows a relationship to become intense. However, in order for a relationship

_____

_____

_____

to become intense and profound, activities must be shared. In other words, we may reside with a person, sharing meals, a bedroom, and a bathroom. There may be intense moments over time, but it is sharing activities and our entire life with that person that will cause the relationship to become profound. We will evolve together and grow closer rather than farther apart. Experiences that may be often viewed as trivial are deep and meaningful with the right person. Sharing breakfast, taking a walk, and planning a trip are all important and meaningful experiences to share. The destination is not important; it is the journey that matters.

"You love me very well."

"Profound love can endure for a long time when it maintains romantic intensity... while significantly advancing the personal flourishing of each partner."

PsychologyToday.com 25th February, 2014

Even discussing this idea is a wonderfully overwhelming experience. By being aware of and accepting each other's faults at the beginning of a relationship, and knowing they are not going to change, we can focus on nurturing and growing. However, not accepting a person and expecting them to change once they are in the relationship can turn into an abusive situation. Your response to a situation shows strength. For example, if your partner says something disagreeable in a social setting, your response is not an aggressive one; rather, you give yourself time to think about the situation and then approach it later. You must always have your partner's

_____

_____

_____

best interest in mind, even when he/she says things that may hurt. A nurturing love will work things out. Love is not always pretty.

Another observation I have made in the past is that Joanne and David have both kept their opinions to ourselves when out in public with former partners. They have made this choice to avoid being confronted at home about speaking their mind while at social gatherings. We keep our thoughts and opinions to ourselves in such settings because we do not feel safe with the way our partner may respond.

The balancing point between our inner and outer listening is the heart. This is the meeting point between yourself and another. The position changes to a more outside location when we feel threatened or insecure because we will not let in the threat. The position changes to a more inward location when we feel trust and closeness, as we want to take in the feelings. The position of our listening needs to change in order to be understood. Our listening may begin with an inward position, but if little connection is made or it is a send and receive only conversation, then the position will turn outward until the listener turns off. If we are able to quiet our minds sufficiently and be patient, are we able to listen to all that is there? Are we able to listen to all that is said, and to all that is not said?

By stilling the world around or inside us, we are able to listen more deeply to each other. There are endless possibilities for living. Not everyone notices. If we neglect to listen, and if we fail to really try to understand, we will miss the opportunities and the possibilities to fully know our partner. Our partners are waiting for us to stop so we can meet them

———————————————————————————————

———————————————————————————————

———————————————————————————————

together. We must engage in two-way communication, rather than one sender and one receiver.

In recognizing a life, our own or others, we become conscious or aware of that life. From that moment on we can keep the truth visible of who that person (or person's life) is. This requires constant interest in your partner, but it is not a chore. When we listen and communicate in an authentic manner, we will not encounter the question, "Why didn't you tell me?" Instead, we share the phrase, "I am here for you." In honouring yourself, don't hide those parts of your soul that are more present — keep the truth of who you are visible and clear. Maintain your authenticity in a relationship. Do not try to become your partner, nor should your partner try to change you. Conversely, don't make your partner become you.

Listening to ourselves and to each other requires a constant effort. Listening allows us to open ourselves together in such a way that we can be in tune to the mysteries and wonders that surround us.

It's not always easy to communicate with each other. However, it is always worth it. If we don't feel safe in sharing, taking risks, and travelling together, we will give up on the relationship. The closer and deeper we know a person, the better chance we will have of gauging what their response may be. Even when we are unsure of what their response may be, we may still feel safe with it.

We usually need more than one attempt to fully understand each other and the mysteries that surround us. If we are able to listen with our entire

_____

_____

_____

being, then we will be able to merge with the being of others and be drawn closer to another (person). We also need to listen to all that is not said. Take notice of facial expressions, breathing, and body language. If someone cannot look you in the eye when talking to you, they may need more space and understanding. Know your partner's reactions, such as what a flushed face, a raised eyebrow, or an eye-twitch might mean.

In order to listen reliably, always return to what matters and communicate the idea that "I am here for you". Set aside any preconceptions, personal opinions, and ego so that we can listen to each other. Listening involves far more than just using our ears. It also involves absorbing anything which may be revealed at any given moment with our body, being, and heart.

> *"When a specific fundamental frequency is created by any other object in the neighborhood of the original object, the original object responds to that frequency and that response is called resonance."*
>
> *Oxford Dictionary of Physics*
>
> *"A soul connection is a resonance between two people who respond to the essential beauty of each other's individual natures, behind their facades, and who connect on this deeper level. This kind of mutual recognition provides the catalyst for a potent alchemy. It is a sacred alliance whose purpose is to help both partners discover and realize their deepest potentials. While a heart connection lets us appreciate those we love just*

_____

_____

_____

*as they are, a soul connection opens up a further dimension
— seeing and loving them for who they could be, and for whom
we could become under their influence. This means recognizing
that we both have an important part to play in helping each
other become more fully who we are... A soul connection not only
inspires us to expand, but also forces us to confront whatever
stands in the way of that expansion."*

John Welwood

There is a soul-connection, a desire to nurture your partner through growth by seeing and loving the person they could become in the relationship. The benefit also works in our favour, as we can see and love the person we ourselves are capable of becoming in a relationship. This is done by nurturing, supporting, and encouraging our partner to grow. When presented with a question or idea from our partner, we may simply respond with, "Why not?" Why not try this new thing? Why not learn a new skill or take a class? We need to remember that if our partner changes his/her mind about this new adventure, that we must not press them into doing something they do not want to do.

We always offer support to each other, for things large or small. If one wants to further his or her education, the other responds with a 'Why not, and how can I help you?'

Resonance is not created by us. It emerges when we tap into the underlying rhythm and flow of the universe. It can be felt as a physical level of

_____

_____

_____

connection, facilitated by vibrational exchange that operates constantly, whether or not we are communicating verbally or are even aware of its existence. The word resonance means "re-sound", which indicates a flow of vibration between two things — in this case two people. Resonance can be the momentary upwelling of three tightly interwoven events: first, a sharing of one or more positive emotions between you and another; second, a synchronous event or events that occur between your partner and yourself; and third, a reflected motive to invest in each other's well-being that brings about mutual care.

Resonance is the kind of experience that we perceive as connection with another person. We can think of it as love or as one of the foundations of love.

In modern Western societies, the relationship commitment institutional-ized in marriage is generally initiated because of experiences of positive resonance between two people. The person you want to build a life with is someone with whom you experience an emotional connection, a resonance.

In the beginning of an intimate relationship, instances of resonance often seem easy to come by. Once you are sharing day-to-day life with someone these instances of resonance may become less frequent. Infatuation mellows into something less intense. Often this happens simply because one or both people stop trying to create or pay attention to shared emotional moments. This is where complacency occurs. Couples take for granted that the other will always be there for them, regardless of how much the other partner may be neglected. There always seems to be

———————————————————————————

———————————————————————————

———————————————————————————

something else to do, something perceived as more important. This causes us to give up — we give up trying, asking, and suggesting. We give up to a point where we are enduring and maintaining our relationship rather than living and thriving in it. In more extreme situations, couples can get into an argument over who is going to get acceptance and acknowledgment from the other, which erodes the investment in each other's wellbeing. For example, it may not be helpful to focus on which person's job is worth more in terms of either recompense or recognition.

Although a lack of instances of positive resonance may not erode the commitment you make to your relationship, it can make it harder to remember what made you want to make the commitment in the first place. It certainly makes the relationship considerably less enjoyable and desirable.

One common problem is that different people connect with feelings, their own and others', *via different paths.* One person's idea of a setting conducive to positive resonance might be a tangible, more materialistic path such as an elegant dinner with flowers and soft music, or one pertaining to social expectations such as making a commitment to a relationship only after receiving a diamond ring. However, another person might feel the resonance arise after climbing a mountain to watch the sunrise. As resonance is a shared experience, a setting that promotes resonance must do so for both people in the relationship. This doesn't necessarily mean that both people need to have the exact same experience. One person might be swept up in admiration or empathetic excitement for a partner's experience. However, the experience has to resonate back and forth between both partners.

_____

_____

_____

Communication from morning to night is important. Everything from 'Good morning, bright eyes' to 'Good night, and God bless' and all that is in between needs to be said or expressed. When listening for understanding, be present. This allows the other to feel safe.

Moments of resonance are important to having the kind of experience most of us desire in a committed, intimate relationship. They can't be manufactured, but they can be cultivated. When the time is right, moments of resonance (which are always there) will present themselves.

"As we were standing in the snow, by a river, a magical moment of resonance presented itself. It was a point of realisation, when I knew that my path was changing. Looking back on this path, if one little thing had not occurred, we would not be where we are now." ~ David

> *"Love is more than just a powerful feeling. Without the commitment, it is mere infatuation. Without the passion, it is mere dedication. Without nurturing, even the best can wither and die."*
>
> *Julian Baggini*

> *The weather is on our side.*
>
> *tpb*

Fortunately for David and Joanne, they were favoured by snowy days and closed roads which allowed them time and opportunity to realise what a loving, caring, and nurturing relationship actually feels like. In literal terms David and Joanne experienced a snowy day. Figuratively speaking, the weather being on our side means that the universe is providing us with all that we need.

If we are in communication with the universe, then we are communicating with thoughts, feelings, and vibrations, inside and out. We control ourselves in the communication. We control our happiness/sadness. We do not control all events that happen, but in controlling how we react to these events, we are able to control our happiness. When we are happy, our vibrations increase, and when our vibrations increase, we attract people and events to better our lives.

When such an event such as a snowy day comes upon us and we are provided with quality time to spend with a special person, we are able to nurture and grow our relationship.

_____

_____

_____

SOMETHING TO CHEW ON...

1. Have you ever experienced love at first sight? If so, how did the events unfold?

2. When sharing experiences with your partner, how much of the experience shared is yours? Is the experience shared 50/50, 25/75, 75/25? Do you enjoy your partner's ideas as much as they enjoy yours?

3. How do you respond to your partner's faults? Is there a way to improve upon your response?

4. What does the phrase "You love me very well" mean to you?

5. Do you feel a resonance in your relationship? What form does this resonance take? Is this resonance openly shared?

6. What have you noticed about how you feel when you accept that you are not in control of events that are happening?

_____

_____

_____

THE MUSIC OF THE SPHERES BURSTS FORTH

As told by Holt the Yak...

Too few live the life that
the universe
allows.
tpb

It is unlikely that we will perish for want of information or knowledge, but rather for a want of appreciation. We often do not appreciate knowledge, information, or each other. As a society, we appreciate less every successive generation. For example, we may not appreciate genuine quality time for ourselves and others as well as the natural environment around us. There are small things to be grateful for on a daily basis, such as waking up, a smile, our health — these things are often overlooked as we go about a busy but empty life.

An expression of gratitude or appreciation is a simple task and would seem to be an inherently human trait. However, it seems as if gratitude is sliding out of our daily lives. This may be due to our fast-paced, distracted lifestyle. This frenetic lifestyle makes it very easy to overlook gratitude. If we are grateful (and we choose to express this gratitude) for the events that occur, our lives will become richer. Many individuals are not able to receive things gratefully (be they material, such as a gift; or non-material, such as a compliment). Socially, we have been programmed by our society to view giving as important. Taking is not important but receiving is important. To receive a compliment, a gift, or help takes both humility and grace. In being able to humbly receive, we can let our gratitude flow out. Our gratitude does not have to be cultivated, for a gratitude that is cultivated is of little significance. In order to genuinely express gratitude, we do not always even need to speak — our gratitude can be expressed with a look or a touch.

People who withdraw behind their technology or who consider themselves to be at the centre of all things will find they miss out on the whole process of life — it will simply pass them by while they are wrapped up in their own closed world. If you can genuinely express gratitude you will also find yourself more receptive to things that come your way. This will allow you to enjoy and thrive on the experiences that life has to offer.

Why is it that we appreciate less? Is our unappreciation driven from an internal or external source? Externally, technological development — cell phones, laptops, etc. — are a major factor that is essentially enabling the

_____

_____

_____

withdrawal of people from society. As people rely more and more on their devices, they gain a dependence on them, and this dependency draws them away from genuine social interactions. For example, a couple at a coffee shop may be in each other's physical presence, but their constant texting on their phones means that not a word is exchanged.

As mentioned earlier, we do not lack a will to believe things but a will to wonder about things. To wonder, was, in the opinion of Descartes, one of the passions of the soul. A passion, according to Descartes, is an emotion that consists of a "passion" with regard to the subject to which it happens, and an "action" with regard to that which makes it happen. Wonder, according to Descartes, is the product of the first encounter with an object, and thus the first passion (e.g. esteem or contempt, generosity or pride, humility or abjectness) offers two possible courses. The pleasures of the world, according to Descartes, are dependent on the proper exercise of the passions (emotions), as are all of the world's evils if they are misused. In the end, true wisdom is to master our passions such that the evils can be turned into a source of joy.

People want to believe and have a need to believe, so the want is not lacking. However, if we do not have a solid foundation, we will believe anything. Beliefs can be very difficult to change. For example, after having a struggle with church beliefs, I did not trash the belief system — they were adapted to allow survival and growth. The will to believe, based on one's own thoughts, is also being lost due to the many distractions life has to offer — particularly electronic ones which are so symptomatic of the

_____

_____

_____

modern world. We are either afraid or don't want to wonder — we want to be fed. "Tell me what I want", or "Tell me what I need." This need is amply catered to by our modern consumer society. For example, alcohol is used as an off switch. The very thing that feeds these wants is the very thing that needs turning off, for example the need to escape from life by immersing oneself into a video game. Another prime example is a diet of fast or poor-quality food. You start to crave it and can't do without it, and yet this desire for fast food needs to be turned off in order to preserve your physical and mental health.

Natural wonders are all around us. Consider stars, the movement of the celestial bodies, and a sunset. Each of these spheres has its own vibrations (music) which depends on its size.

Listening opens the door to everything that matters. We listen to awaken our heart and by listening deeply we are able to become vital and more alive. In listening to ourselves, we can be overcome by uncertainty — fear of the unknown, fear of rejection, or fear of putting our feelings out there. For example, we may fear crying in public or even laughing out loud in public. There is always a fear of showing emotions.

People have considerable difficulty in dealing with intensity. Once intensity reaches a level of around eighty-five per cent, people tend to shut off. In this manner, authentic emotions are not dealt with. On the other hand, people can watch a Hollywood movie where people are blown apart and not bat an eyelid. As David witnessed a lady falling down a flight of stairs, several people behind her turned and almost fled back up the stairs rather than offer any assistance. This is an interesting example of people's limits when it comes to responding to real-life intensity. We need to "accept the risk". In order to accept this risk, we need to be authentic or true to ourselves. At this point (of authenticity) we are able to be present and to live in the moment — the only moment there is, even though this moment is made up of both the past and future as well as the present.

Life is full of uncertainty (things we have no control over), and when we are awake we are open to the risks of being both vulnerable and honest. If we fail to recognise our uncertainties, they can cause anxiety. Many people are pushed by their anxiety to rely on someone or something else external to help correct the problem. An alternative approach would be to look at the problem and find the internal solution. This would rely on neither medications nor other external influences. This would bring a long-lasting solution to the anxiety problem.

We can replace our expectations with plans. While we are able to plan for and guide our future, we cannot control the exact outcomes. Rather than thinking that the future will provide you with exactly what you want, think about what you can do to create the sorts of experiences that you want to have. Part of what makes uncertainty difficult is the lack of control that uncertainty brings. If you plan for (or at least anticipate) the possibilities that may occur, this will help ease the anxiety associated with uncertainty. Ask yourself: "What's the worst that can happen?" Thinking about the worst-case scenario can often reduce anxiety. Instead of worrying or obsessing about life's uncertainties, focus on those things that you can

_____

_____

_____

control. Focusing on the small things you can control will allow you to take a step back, breathe, relax, and calmly move forward. If you are unduly worried about the myriad of uncertainties that will unfold as time passes, you will not notice or appreciate the moment you are in.

Listening to ourselves and our needs allows us to eventually be open to knowing what others also need. This openness allows us to communicate. We often transmit more information than we receive. Perhaps this is due to an overabundance of information in our lives. By listening and opening our hearts, we are able to improve ourselves and grow. If we decide to accept this risk, the risk of being hurt, we are able to live life fully — we are being here in the moment.

Do time and timelessness move in and out of our hands? Do we feel time-lessness passing through our hands or lives? If we slow our breathing, heart rate, metabolism, and thoughts, then we can slow down time and feel timelessness. Time is something we experience (or think of) as being linear. Time, however, is quite illusory. Because time is related to change, in our modern world time appears to be greatly speeded up. If we did not perceive this change, then perhaps we would not perceive time. For example, a few years ago David was away on a wilderness survival course in northern British Columbia. The second half of the course saw the course candidates dropped in the middle of nowhere with no watch. Other than knowing if it was day or night (the continuous cycle that we use to measure the passage of time!) there was no other way to perceive time — the days and nights were, in and of themselves, timeless. Another way in which

_____

_____

_____

David and Joanne have noticed a sense of timelessness is by doing things together. Things done together can be something as simple as going for a walk, or something more in depth such as writing this book.

We view time in a relative fashion. The past only exists as a memory; it is not real. The future may be a hope or a dream. The past and the future only exist in our minds. In this linear way, however, we create time. As we create time, so we can create timelessness. All we need to do is turn off the part of ourselves that sees the outside world of change. That part of us that is the inner observer can then start to perceive the timelessness and stillness that is constantly within us. If we can thus see both time and timelessness, we can live in a balanced state. This is a state where we are fully present.

If we are aware of the timeless nature of the universe, we can be expanded and grow as we experience moments of wonder, mystery, and love. As these wonders unfold we may become aware of the inner nature of things. The inner nature of living things is constantly emanating, and if we are sufficiently relaxed we will be able to see and hear these emanations. By listening openly to the sounds of the universe we are able to alter our experience of life.

Every time we walk or bike in a natural environment, such as a forest, the mountains, or a beach, we slow down. We become aware of ourselves and our environment, which we become a part of. This is why it's important to take the time to experience these locations together, on a regular basis. While on vacation to New Zealand, David and Joanne noticed how they

_____

_____

_____

were drawn to a particular small historic town. The vibration of this space was what they needed to relax and recover from a long journey. This seems simple, but we often neglect to pay attention to these wonderfully simple gifts that life has to offer.

We are connected to something larger than ourselves. We are connected to the power of the universe, and perhaps our own spirituality. After listening with our complete self, we become aware of a higher being that is something more powerful than ourselves. When watching a sunrise or being in the mountains or forests, you become aware that you are part of something infinitely larger than yourself. A loving relationship can invoke the same feelings, as being in a nurturing relationship will cause us to experience a power that is greater than ourselves. The sum of the whole becomes greater than its parts. We can move outside of our own narrow confines and experience an expanded reality, one that can be shared with a loved one. When you are experiencing an event, such as a sunrise, or a loved one's first smile of the day, your mind is calm and quiet and you are fully present and immersed in that moment. We can let ourselves experience and appreciate the mystery or wonder of such an event. We can enter into the mystery without fearing it. As we grow and change together with our partner, fear of the unknown is lessened because we are more aware of a more powerful existence than our individual self. This may be nature, the universe, and God: in short, this is a belief system.

"For where the mind is, there is the treasure."

From the Gospel of Mary

_____

_____

_____

"The mind" is the true and natural self where the heart is also. We find our peace when we realise that peace is within us.

Music can be found everywhere, and it surrounds us all the time. Music amplifies the energy around us and opens up a seemingly infinite number of possibilities that await us in a live well-lived. We yearn for possibilities such as love, happiness, success, and a shared life. Instead of rushing to work, purchasing consumer items, or replacing life with distractions (which are all illusory in terms of maximizing life), slow down and participate with and in life. If you can live in this way, you may find that the music you radiate is vast and rich. All lovers who have lived life to the fullest are aware of the wager that love is stronger than death. The faithfulness of their two hearts resonating across space and time forms a channel or flow of energy. Compassion, wisdom, and creativity are able to flow along this path, thereby allowing us to grow. A life well-lived constitutes growth as we move from experience to experience.

Adversities that are overcome add to this life. Obstacles on life's journey can be used to grow and to attain oneness, closeness, and resilience. Without adversity, there can be no easier path — both are required to give life its full and considerable depth. No matter what adversities we encounter, our decisions and reactions will ultimately determine the outcome. Adversity is part of our lives. Sometimes there is a lot, sometimes there is only a little, but adversity is always there. We can use adversity to improve our lives, depending on how we treat it and react to it. Adversity has the power to strengthen us emotionally as what was once the feared "unknown"

_____

_____

_____

becomes the "known". Adversity can educate us about our limits, our lack of control of the world around us, or a character flaw or weakness. We can use adversity as a teacher. In learning the lessons adversity has to offer, we become a stronger person.

If we are aware that our vibrations are not in tune with our surroundings, it may be an indicator that our health is being affected. When we are suffering from illness, our vibrations may not be on the same frequency as they would be if we were healthy. Animals can sense when another animal is sick, weak, or vulnerable. As humans, we are (we can be) aware of others who are not spiritually, physically, and mentally healthy.

Other people may hear, feel, or sense our music. Sometimes they want to avoid it, for it is too intense or unfamiliar, and sometimes they want to be a part of it. For example, one day Joanne and David met for coffee in a small town on Vancouver Island. They gave each other a hug and kiss and then placed their order. As they were sitting there, a woman kept looking over and smiling at them. When they got up to leave, she approached Joanne and commented on the "rendezvous kiss" (as she described it) and how great it all was! Clearly the music was there not only for David and Joanne, but for others as well. Another personal example David and Joanne observed was after they had spent an afternoon in a local coffee shop working on this book. As they were about to leave, two young women looked and smiled at Joanne as she got on her motorbike to leave. They were obviously chatting about the small woman in front of them getting on a large motorbike. Clearly, although they were spectators in the moment, they were enjoying the moment itself and looked as they would very much have liked to be getting on motorbikes of their own and riding off.

People with whom we have no particular relationship can be drawn to our music. We can be the source of our own music or it simply passes through us. We can even share brief experiences with people whom we have no other relationship with. For example, if we're experiencing a particularly difficult day and need to restore our positive energy, we may take a walk in the forest. Upon entering the forest, our vibrations may be at one level, but then be changed upon exit, as we have restored the balance of our vibrations through being connected to nature. Others in the same environment may be emitting the same vibrations.

_____

_____

_____

SOMETHING TO CHEW ON...

1. How often do you find yourself wondering about the world and your place within it?

2. Have you ever found yourself too exhausted to question the news and been merely content to be fed the information? Have you ever found yourself doing the same with the ingredients of the food you eat?

3. When confronted with an intense situation, how do you typically respond?

4. List three things that you would consider to be larger than yourself. What is your connection to each of these things?

5. What is the "treasure of the mind?"

6. Do you ever find yourself drawn to people with whom you have no particular relationship for reasons you are not able to readily identify? Think about what these reasons may be. Are they part of something larger than yourself?

_____

_____

_____

TO MAKE FRIENDS
WITH A CORPSE

As told by Holt the yak...

All things desired are on the other side of our insecurities.
tpb

Our fear of letting go of our possessions (including people) feeds our insecurities and uncertainties. This disallows us to grow. We become cold superficial beings who are lost in our own field of material objects. We become insecure with the belief that we need to hold on to objects and people who fail to allow us to grow and flourish.

According to Thomas Merton, "freedom" generally means "choice freedom" — i.e. I can do what I want, purchase what I desire, etc. These "free" choices are often driven by the cultural conditioning of a society and are materially driven by an individual's compulsive wants (probably not "needs"). An example of cultural conditioning would be a Christian-based society which celebrates Christmas. Even though people may not be Christians themselves, they will still take part in seasonal festivities because they are under the misguided comprehension that this is how things should be done.

> *"The freedom that matters is the ability to be in touch with the centre of your being."*
>
> *Thomas Merton*

External, material objects may include a new phone, a large house, unnecessary things in the large house, and a collection of cars. These things absolutely will not allow the growth and profundity of a relationship. They may even hinder growth as they are such a distraction. For example, we have experienced the big flat screen television used as "background noise" which distances us from people. This is exacerbated even further if you are not being listened to in the first place. The message that we receive as a result of this is "I don't want to talk to you or listen to you. I don't want to hear about your day." Internal, non-material experiences must be shared with our significant other in order for each person to grow as an individual and thus allow the relationship to grow and maintain health.

There is no profundity in material objects. Soon after opening the package, the intensity fades. This is much like the short-lived intensity of superficial encounters, or brief, intense relationships. There is a lack of depth because little is shared, there is no giving/receiving, and there is no intention of growing together. If we only rely on objects for fulfilment, then we will be disappointed because there is always a new and improved object on the market. We look for fulfilment in objects by comparing them with other objects. We compare our objects to other people's objects and thus perpetuate our own misery. This may also cause us to compare our own relationship to those of others, especially if we view our spouse as an object or as an extension of our self rather than as an individual. There is less energy required to purchase material objects than that required to actually work on a relationship, and so possessions may be used in a relationship in an effort to recharge us. If we have much, we may feel prosperous and successful; if we do not, then we may not. The fact that material possessions can be transitory for the most part tends to make these emotions transitory and also somewhat illusory.

We cannot put quality time into a material possession and expect our relationship with people to flourish. Quality time must be spent with people in order to grow.

> *"Attachment to matter gives rise to a passion without an image of itself. It is drawn from sources that are contrary to higher nature."*
>
> *The Gospel of Mary*

The passion has no image because matter is a tangible, material object with no spiritual aspect.

> *"We are what we have."*
>
> *Gary Morson*

_____

_____

_____

Due to the illusory nature of possessions, we knowingly or unknowingly tend to regard our possessions as part of ourselves. Because we have such a fragile sense of self, we need support for this self and an attachment to material possessions can help to provide this support. Our fragile self can be caused by a lack of support and nurturing, abuse, or the influences of others. We may not have peace with ourselves or be comfortable with ourselves. For example, we may not be confident if we are not wearing a certain style of clothes. This is an example of our giving possessions the power to give us confidence. The "power dresser" relies on these possessions (the clothes) and in doing so gives the possessions power. Perhaps people who have never had to do anything without the aid or support of possessions don't actually realise that they can function without these possessions which have become a dependence. For example, four thousand calories of food a day may be consumed and seem necessary for fulfilment; however, it is not necessary to eat this much. We give our possessions the power to give us confidence.

There are three states of our existence: having, doing, and being (Sartre, 1956). These states are each potentially critical to self-definition: what a person calls me and what they call mine can be a difficult distinction to make. We feel and act about certain things that are ours much the same as we feel and act about ourselves. Our fame, our children, and the work of our hands may be as dear to us as our bodies are, and they may arouse the same feelings and the same acts of reprisal if attacked. And are our bodies simply ours, or are they *us*? When we treat a person as a possession, we take on their achievements as our own. In reverse, if a parent feels as if

———————————————————————————————

———————————————————————————————

———————————————————————————————

they have failed on their own education or sporting prowess, they may push very hard for their children to succeed and thus treat them as a possession.

The particular possessions we primarily see as part of ourselves show a close relationship to the objects we see as most magical — such objects act as reminders and confirmers of our identity, and that this identity may often reside more in these objects than it does in ourselves. The feeling of identity invested in material objects can be very high. The car for example — a new car is a part of the ego of an individual. A shiny new car is experienced very much as a shiny new self.

Our possessions make up who we are, and in doing so, do we become our possessions or do we become our own possession? If we and our possessions are viewed as part of the same whole, does that whole become us? We would tend to see others this way and we would assume they see us in this manner also. This can become markedly more pronounced for those people whose confidence relies on their possessions. This may in turn lead to either people gathering a false impression of us, or to others gathering the impression that we want them to have of us. This would depend on the situation, environment, and observer. The desire for "more and better" will push this along. "Me" refers to the self and "Mine" refers to the possession we identify with. If we can't do without the "mine", then "me" and "mine" will in fact become one and the same. We may have learned this as early as childhood. We may have inadvertently or deliberately been taught this by our parents.

_____

_____

_____

The relationships between having, doing, and being are strong. Sartre (1956) suggests that doing is a transitional state or a manifestation of the more fundamental desires to have or to be. Further, Sartre maintains that the only reason we want to have something is to enlarge our sense of self, and that the only way we can know who we are is by observing what we have. In other words, having and being are distinct but inseparable. A good example of this is getting an education — we have to study in order to become well-educated. In other words, we take action to obtain what we want. Actions are bridges between having and being. The bridge depends on the being. When an object becomes a possession, what were once self and not-self are joined together. At this point having and being merge. Thus, according to Sartre, possessions are all-important to knowing who we are. We seek, express, confirm, and ascertain our sense of being through what we have.

Our possessions can become "the prize". Time and effort are put into them at the expense of our relationships.

Csikszentmihalyi (1982) explains:

> "A person who owns a nice home, a new car, good furniture, the latest appliances, is recognized by others as having passed the test of personhood in our society. ...the objects we possess and consume are...wanted because...they tell us things about ourselves that we need to hear in order to keep ourselves from falling apart. This information includes the social recognition

> *that follows upon the display of status symbols, but it includes*
> *also the much more private feedback provided by special*
> *household objects that objectify a person's past, present, and*
> *future, as well as his or her close relationships."*

Olson (1981, 1985) found that young couples cited favourite objects in the home that reflected their future plans and goals, while older couples cited objects related to their experiences together as a couple. Memories are part of us, and so the memories and possessions can become part of us. We may still have memories without the possessions. Triggers, such as a photo (a possession in and of itself), will help us remember past events.

Our obsession with material possessions can affect our ability to have meaningful relationships. Perhaps when we compare ourselves to others, we may notice that they have similar or desired objects, thus causing us to want a relationship with those people. On the other hand, if others have different, undesirable, or no objects, we may not give those people a second look.

A lack of material possessions may confer a lack of success; in this society, this is very likely. The person with the nice house in a nice neighbourhood and the new car(s) may be viewed as successful. However, a person who lives by simple means and is happy with life may not be seen as successful, compared to the former. For example, I have seen these two oddballs do a lot of walking, regardless of the weather. When they are out walking in the rain, they get looks from passing drivers and passengers which are

_____

_____

_____

very clearly saying, "Oh, those poor people can't afford a car", when the very simple truth is that they just like walking in the rain!

As pertaining to Festinger's social comparison theory (1954), we compare ourselves with others because we naturally want accurate self-evaluations. We may, for example, compare our abilities to those of others. If we practice swimming, we may perhaps watch other swimmers and compare our skills to theirs. We will naturally observe a swimmer whose ability is lesser than ours. This comparison will cause us to feel better about our own ability. We may be able to evaluate our progress in doing so. In turn, we will observe a swimmer whose ability is greater than ours. This comparison will allow us to see that there is room for improvement.

By following this same social comparison theory, we will also compare our possessions to those of other people. We may compare our car to the cars of others. If our car is new, expensive, and flashy, then we will feel better, more successful perhaps, than a person who drives a common mid-range car. However, when we encounter a person driving a flashier car than ours, we may tend to believe that we would feel happier if only we have that flashier car.

It seems that possessions are expected to fill that role that is not provided by a loving partner. The expectation may not be a conscious one. When we feel an emptiness, we often look to consume.

Happiness ultimately comes from within — the accumulation of material possessions can have the same effect as an embargo response to the life that goes on around us. For example, we may think we are happy, but our mind and body will tell us otherwise. We may say this life is great, but we're morbidly obese because we're trying to consume enough to make us feel better.

Purchases we make can have effects far beyond the actual purchase itself and the ephemeral illusion of happiness a new purchase provides. For example, David's purchase of a flat black, classic styling Triumph motorbike has deeper effects and meaning than the purchase itself. The purchase also provided another avenue for shared experiences (motorcycling together) and it is also a trigger for experiences past. A string of possessions is still attached to the experience of the original possession. Whenever David goes to the range or goes hunting, he can clearly remember excitedly buying his first rifle many years ago.

Images are also very important to people. Often these images have little to do with the reality of a situation. For example, images associated to a biker may include a motorcycle, a leather jacket, and tattoos. He may or may not ride a motorcycle. Images associated to a mountaineer may include hiking boots, travel clothes, and GORE-TEX. She may or may not hike much. Images associated to a scholar include a book collection, a pipe, a bad haircut, and patches on the elbows of his jacket. He may or may not read much. Images associated to a vegan/liberal/enviro-friendly person may include natural fibre clothing, unwashed hair, sandals, MacBook, and Starbucks coffee. Another example is the liberal social justice warrior which is a mask many hide behind. They don't look at their own mess but

_____

_____

_____

concern themselves with herd-like mentality as they push their own social agenda, whatever it may be, at any given moment. Considerable importance can be attached to these images — as much as that which is attached to material possessions. However, when the sun goes down and the image is put to rest for the day, it is apparent that these images are as ephemeral as material possessions when it comes to happiness.

To prevent yourself from becoming obsessed by and identifying yourself too strongly with your possessions, other avenues will allow you to continue to grow and develop both as an individual and as a partner.

Allow yourself to explore the world around you. Nurturing your curiosities and allowing yourself to wonder at the world around you are two of the best ways to make yourself a more aware individual. Activities which allow you to wonder and explore can significantly expand your horizons and help you see new perspectives. Getting out of your comfort zone can help you to develop and allow you to see things from a different point of view.

Trying new activities that interest you or even activities that someone has invited you to join will diversify your experiences. Even if you don't end up enjoying yourself, you will still be more informed and versatile than you were prior to trying this new activity. Be open-minded to trying new activities, even if they don't initially seem very appealing. For example, while not overly fond of winter (or the term "snow bunny"!), Joanne was nonetheless willing to go to the mountains with David to try skiing and snowshoeing because years ago, a friend asked her "Why not?" Seeing

_____

_____

_____

a sport, hobby, or interest through another person's eyes can give you a new appreciation of that sport, hobby or interest.

Travel whenever you can. There is a vast amount you can learn from other places, especially foreign countries and cultures. Travel experiences will expose you to different perspectives, histories, and opinions. Travel will show you that the world, even if it's a nearby town, is multifaceted and can add new sides to you, too. Domestic travel is also an excellent way to experience different culture and variety. For example, if you are on the west coast of Canada, you might be surprised to know that the lifestyle on the east coast is quite different. *Make sure to get off the beaten path when you travel.* After all, why would you bother to travel from Canada to Europe and stay there in a Best Western Hotel when you could have a far more enriching experience staying in a small rural B & B with a local family?

Meet new people. Every person has their own views, reality, and opinions that are formed on the basis of their experiences. New people can expose you to new information. In order to meet new people, you should first acknowledge that your reality is not the only or right reality. Reality differs for everyone.

_____

_____

_____

SOMETHING TO CHEW ON...

1. How would you make the distinction between "me" and "mine"?

2. Consider the importance ascribed to material possessions. With that importance in mind, is it likely that we become our possessions, or do we become our own possession?

3. Consider a possession you have acquired. Does it in any way help you to maintain or project your identity? Would you be a different person without that particular possession?

_____

_____

_____

IT'S NOTHING BUT
IT'S EVERYTHING

As told by Holt the Yak....

You cannot rescue people
From their past.
You can merely stand at their side for the present.
tpb

I like this particular tpb because it tells me that we must do our best to understand our partner's past in order to stand with them. If we do this, we can see boundaries, statements, or no reactions, and understand why and where they are coming from. Then we can respond accordingly with empathy, or else simply avoid the situation. The choice is always ours. Therefore, we must be comfortable/brave enough to share our past with our loved ones, especially when our past is pertinent to a difficult situation.

As we die and the elements we are made of will join the elements that were here before us and the ones that will exist after we die, we will feel the being of all eternity.

In order to feel the being of eternity we need to distance ourselves from the view that eternity is time-dependent. As mentioned in Chapter Three, we should get in touch with timelessness. Consider how quickly time can pass when you are with a loved one or doing something that you really enjoy. In these situations, time simply does not matter. This being the case, it would seem that our sense of time (passing) varies according to how we feel at any given moment. For example, if we are in a happy and contented state, time will fly by. Conversely, in a sad state, time tends to slow down and drag.

With this in mind, we can see that the "being of all eternity", our spiritual life that will continue after death, does not experience time. Our spiritual life is timeless and experiences a change of state or being upon our death.

> *"Death is not an event in life: we do not live to experience death. If we take eternity to mean not infinite temporal duration, but timelessness, then eternal life belongs to those who live in the present. Our life has no end in the way in which our visual field has no limits."*
>
> *Ludwig Wittgenstein*

_____

_____

_____

To perceive this, we need to believe in a higher power. We also need to acknowledge this higher power with our partner. We don't have to share exactly the same belief, but we need to grow together with our beliefs. This will allow us to move together in beliefs, based on a genuine desire to know our partner more deeply, thus becoming more intertwined. Joanne and David grew up with different theological influences. David attended church regularly. As an infant, Joanne was baptised in a Greek Orthodox church, and following that, she had never set foot in a church for anything other than weddings and funerals. Since being in a nurturing relationship with David, Joanne has become genuinely interested in his practical approach to theology, an area where she previously had no interest. Similarly, David has benefitted from reading books based on Buddhist philosophies which influenced Joanne during her life in Korea. Neither of them discussed doing this. They simply formed an actual interest in the other's beliefs concerning an important subject.

Although we are living in the present, we are the past/present/future. This makes us complete. If we feel the being of all eternity, then we are experiencing a connection with something larger than ourselves. This allows us to participate in life rather than merely observe life through others. It also allows one to take responsibility for his or her actions, instead of indirectly blaming others for what happens.

We can create ideas or feelings that we believe are larger than ourselves (such as love, fear, hate, and envy) and these can mask what the larger thing actually is. The mask could be seemingly insignificant ("nothing")

_____

_____

_____

but could potentially affect an entire life ("everything"). These masks can drive a person for their whole life. You can live your hate. Hate can consume and control life. An angry divorce or the loss of a loved one can be the driving force behind self-destruction.

These masks can take different forms. They can range from an obvious physical mask (such as dark sunglasses on an overcast day) to an emotional mask which we can hide behind because of fear. For example, if we feel insecure in a social setting, we may hide behind a mask of name-dropping.

Another reason we wear a mask is because we are scared that we will be "found out". We are afraid to show our true selves to the world in case the world says, "Oh, it's only you." However, being "only you" is exactly what you are and nothing to be afraid of. How can you be better than being yourself? Why would you not want to be yourself?

We need to have sufficient courage to shed our masks. If we are to realise our potential, whatever that may be, we will do it better by being ourselves. Wearing a mask can be tiring — we may even forget who we are if we come to rely on our mask for an extended period of time. By wearing a mask we are, in effect, withholding part of ourselves which we deem to be either less worthy or unworthy. Be authentically yourself! Remember, you put the mask on, so you can also take it off.

This feeling as if we are a part of something larger than ourselves can provide the strength necessary to help, communicate, and be with others from any given moment in the present and then on into the future whatever

_____

_____

_____

that may bring. Strength, confidence, and will can allow us to lessen fear, envy, etc. The mask we have created can become thinner and weaker and this will allow us to see the truth of any given situation. These truths may not always be comfortable — that is why we create the mask in the first place. The truth, however, is always the truth.

Inconsequential events can have far-reaching consequences. Acknowledge kindness and don't assume. Keep expectations in check, assess understanding, and express appreciation by simply saying "thank you". Tell your partner you are there for them — and actually meaning it by being there. If this does not come from the heart, it will be felt. Do not become complacent and do not taking your loved one or your loved one's actions for granted. Do things because you want to or because you mean it, rather than because you feel obliged to. Perhaps we should take what our partners say at face value. Keep in mind that tone, facial expressions, and body language can make it difficult to take things at face value. We should take what our partners say as truth and not expect more. This is why constant communication is key. Finally, it is very important to acknowledge a misunderstanding. If this is a sensitive topic, give your partner time to explain what happened. Share how you feel. Discuss how to prevent this from happening again.

If we live mindfully in the present, we are not prevented from making future plans. Living in the present simply means that we are aware that there is no point in losing ourselves in worries and fears concerning the future. Being lost in the future causes fear and this fear can grow into anxiety. This in turn may cause depression and a fear of moving forward.

_____

_____

_____

This leads to the previously mentioned building of masks. We should live in the moment and make simple future plans. If we don't live in the moment and don't make these plans, we will readily find an excuse for not having done so.

David and Joanne currently have two simple plans for the near future — a three-day cross-country ski trip and a five-day hunting trip in the mountains. This will be time well-spent outdoors building depth in their relationship through shared experiences and enjoying the music of nature.

Mindfulness in the present does not prevent us from looking into the past either. We must live in the present. If we try to live in the past our lives will stall and we will be unable to move on. The past provides us with its own mask which does not allow us to see and live in the moment. Ergo, we may not be able to continue to grow. For example, by not getting past a divorce, you may not be able to move on and so will remain in a state of bitter unhappiness. If you are firmly established in the present moment, it is possible to look back deeply at your past. You should not and in fact cannot go back to the past. It existed once, and now it is unreal and shadowy.

The more expectations you have, the less you will become. Create only one expectation at a time. Having fewer expectations allows for a happier life. Having high expectations is not the same as having fewer expectations, however. If we have high expectations for ourselves, we are likely to set ourselves up to realise these expectations. If, however, our expectations are unrealistic, we could be setting ourselves up for failure. An unattainable but

_____

_____

_____

common expectation is the assumption and expectation that our partner understands us or knows what we are thinking or feeling.

You cannot control another's thoughts, but your reaction to those thoughts can affect how they feel about you. For example, you can't reasonably expect your partner to make you happy. However, if you are both happy in yourselves, then you can be happy together. Unhappy people may be on a different page. Because expectations are learned, we are able to change. We can come to agree upon what actually makes us happy, providing we want to continue to remain together. This process will happen naturally and subconsciously, provided that both people are in the same space. Therefore, when unhappiness occurs within a relationship, it's clear that both partners are not in the same space or on the same page regarding a matter. Those expectations that are complicated or which rely on external influences of any kind (i.e. outside of yourself) can set up the future in such a way that it may not meet your needs.

Focus on what is simple.

_____

_____

_____

SOMETHING TO CHEW ON....

1. Consider the difference between participating in life and living a vicarious existence.

2. Look back and reflect on events that have occurred in your life that seemed perfectly innocuous at the time. How did these events turn out to be subsequently significant?

3. What does living mindfully in the present mean to you?

4. What are the simple things in life we can focus on in order to improve our experience of life?

THE LEFT IS THE RIGHT

As told by Holt the Yak......

For every ending,
There is a new beginning
tpb

There is a desire in most people to be rid of the darkness that we all have in our lives, such as a bad relationship, difficulties at work, or health concerns. However, without darkness, there would be no shadows and thus no depth perception. Without any depth perception, how are we able to have a sense of direction or know where we are going or where we don't want to be? We have to be in the right place in our darkness in order to move towards the light and grow. This can be recognising a space to step into, or recognising "a window of opportunity" that will make a change in our life. However, sometimes rock bottom has a basement and it can be very hard to see the light from there. We may have to travel farther through our darkness in order to reach the light. In Aunty Audrey's garage, a place of realisation, the space was there. It is possible to create our own space or share the space with another to create our own opportunity. When the darkness allows us to see, we then become aware of the spaces. These spaces move with us through time — different spaces at different times.

As we need to know or discover our way, instead of bypassing the darkness we can work both with it and through it. David's fear was of dying without having lived well enough. Life is not a time issue, but a quality issue. The inability to control your death may contribute to your fear of it. However, we do control how we live. Therefore, contemplating our own mortality (rather than dismissing or ignoring the idea) can help us to focus on putting energy into transforming and/or healing ourselves rather than being drawn into a vortex of fear and uncertainty.

The present is the only moment there is and therefore also the only truth that we can be certain of. We must be in touch with our past and all of its connections in order to truly experience the present, which of course leads to the future. The past and the future are both part of the present but they are not the place in which we exist. The past is not our home and we have not yet arrived in the future.

When you are able to make two become one, the inside like the outside and the higher like the lower, you will become a complete human being. An integration of these parts can help to anchor yourself at a place (be it a point in time or a place in space) of oneness before any opposites arise. This integration has little to do with what you see, but rather with how you see it, and how you respond to it. If there is a place of balance inside of us

_____

_____

_____

between the finite and the infinite, then we can find our place of oneness. If the finite and infinite are in balance, then energy will flow through us. This energy can affect the state of others around us if they are open to it and are consequently aware of it emanating from us. A relationship exists somewhere between the energy and the balance. A solid relationship will be a symbiotic. This can be as simple as "I will do the washing while you do the vacuuming", or, "Would you like me to prepare the vegetables while you start cooking?" Things do not need to be complicated in order to work!

Often, the relationship will lean one way or the other, depending on what is going on at any given moment. Ideally however, an overall state of balance will exist. A state of balance is well worth working on as it will be sustainable.

It is also important to consider the roles of perception and reality. Our thoughts and feelings seem very real to us and so we tend to conclude that they are real. Perception is the window through which we look to view reality. Our beliefs may also be in contrast to reality. They are a perception of reality rather than reality itself.

Every individual has their own unique reality. The way in which they perceive it may be quite different from the way it is perceived by others. This in no way diminishes the individual's perception of his/her own reality. Perception and reality are shaped by experience. We gain this experience as we travel along our path. If, as you travel along your path, you don't like the way it is going, then you can change your perceptions and your

_____

_____

_____

reality. You are responsible for, and in control of, your story. If you don't like your story, then write a new one. The power to do so is in your hands.

Reality is the true state of things. "Things", by definition, are in and of themselves quite neutral. As we look at reality, we add our own perceptions to the mix. How our reality appears tells us about our perceptions. There is a big overlap between reality and perception.

_____

_____

_____

SOMETHING TO CHEW ON...

1. How does the position of your listening need to be expressed in order to be understood?

2. The past is not our home, but how does it still affect us?

3. What does a symbiotic relationship mean to you?

4. Is there a gap between perception and reality, as well as an overlap? If so, what form does the gap take?

_____

_____

_____

THE UNEXAMINED LIFE
IS NOT WORTH LIVING
—SOCRATES

As told by Holt the Yak....

To observe someone standing before you,
Open and true,
With his or her spirit radiating unhindered,
Is to witness pure love.
tpb

When we allow others the privilege of observing and examining us in our most vulnerable state (whatever that may be), we display our true love and trust in the observer, as no others will see it.

To look at ourselves, to truly examine our own being, is to allow ourselves to grow and improve. To truly examine our own being, we must be honest and objective with ourselves. It can be very difficult to do this and may take more than one honest attempt. If we are aware of both our faults and our virtues, then we can work to nurture that which is worth keeping while letting go of that which is not. Observe, examine, feel, acknowledge. To successfully observe ourselves we must engage in honest self-reflection. As we do this, feelings will come and go. Do not judge yourself for having these feelings, some of which you may consider unworthy. Acknowledge them and let them pass. Do not cling to negative energy and don't allow it to grow. Let go of positive energy in order to allow more to grow in its place. The destructive power of negative energy can be debilitating. Be grateful for what you are and what you have all the time, not just when everything's going right. Gratitude is positive. Be grateful for what is, including life's lessons that you may not necessarily want. This will allow you to let more positive energy into your life. Do not believe bad things happen to you — in this way you will immediately turn yourself into a victim. Consider who or what is to blame when good things happen to you. Do you think or believe that you are solely responsible for these good things? Do you believe that you have worked hard for them to occur? Do you also believe (or blame) that other people or events are responsible for your failures? If so, how is it that when good things happen, they are all because of you, but when bad things happen, they are the fault of another? We need to take responsibility for all of our actions and inactions, as well as for their consequences. By not allowing negativity to flourish and nurturing the positive, you will flourish. Being a positive person (which is not always easy) will allow you to get what you want out of life. Positivity will help you enjoy your life even if things don't go as planned.

_____

_____

_____

"When you realise that everything springs only from yourself, you will learn both peace and joy."

Dalai Lama

Train yourself to stop and look deeply at life. When you look at life, give it more than a superficial glance. It's your life and your stage; give it the thought and attention it deserves. If you fail to look deeply at your life, then your reactions may be such that life will simply pass you by. When you are able to still your mind, you can look at things more deeply. By stilling your mind and quieting the noise, you can closely observe and absorb your surroundings. You can become part of your surroundings rather than being an interloper in them. If you are sharing your surroundings with a loved one, really be there for them — observe and share their spirit and grow together in the moment. Stopping and looking are two aspects of the same thing, and in combination they allow you to examine your life honestly and openly. You can look without stopping and stop without looking. Either way, you will not be getting a full picture. For example, have you ever been hiking in the mountains and looked at the scene before you without stopping? At best you will manage a fleeting glance while your mind is otherwise occupied by not tripping over rocks or tree roots. How much better would the wonder and serenity of the mountains have been if you had both looked and stopped? By stopping and looking, you can immerse yourself in the wonders that surround you. As with the mountains, your experience will be all the richer for the time you took to stop, look, think, examine, and only then move on.

_____

_____

_____

You are able to become part of your environment. You can merge with it. Rather than being a spectator and living a vicarious existence, you can participate in life. Depending on the environment you are in, this can be either a good or bad thing. Life experiences vary according to the choices we make along the way. Deciding which environment we want to be a part of may or may not be an easy choice. Either way, it is still a choice. Your life's journey will be very different depending on your choices of environment. For example, if you choose a life full of negativity such as judgment and blame, you may well end up travelling down a very dark path. If, however, you decide to be in an environment that will help you grow and develop, then many things will be possible. If you find that your chosen environment is dragging you down, make the (sometimes very difficult) decision to change and move on. The difficulties associated with changing the environment that you are in may be time (the right time) and space (having an alternative space to move into). If we are aware of our environment and we change (or adapt), and that changes how people see us, then in turn perhaps we can help others by changing their perception of themselves. You will adapt to suit your environment, just as in the Darwinian process of natural selection. Your environment will not change to suit you no matter how much you want it to or think it should. If we find ourselves in a happy and healthy place, then we are likely to become more like that place.

Just because we may happen to be stuck in a storm does not mean we have to stay there! If you are mired in difficulties or situations that you do not like or that are harming you, then take a different path. You do not

———————————————————————

———————————————————————

———————————————————————

need to stay there. Fear or anxiety can prevent us from changing paths. An honest and open look at your situation and the benefits of changing that situation can help you to gain the courage required to change tack. In this case, being open and honest means that we don't blame ourselves or others; rather, we truly examine the problem and discover its source. Then we consider possible solutions. These solutions are often changes required within ourselves.

On an interpersonal and intrapersonal level, perception can easily allow us to reject our oneness with our surroundings. We become antisocial. We do not go out, and we do not mix or mingle with others. If we judge ourselves harshly or untruly, we begin to isolate ourselves from our surroundings. Often, we are judged by others. Being judged by others can cause fears, anxieties, and stresses to develop and grow. We must realise that we cannot control the thoughts of others. This understanding can be both difficult to realise and difficult to accept. Only by controlling our own thoughts are we able to emerge from this mire. The act of judging often has little or nothing to do with wisdom. The cause-and-effect relationship between judging and being judged is one that escapes most people. This can range anywhere from great to devastating. Judgment can be seen as (and frequently misinterpreted as) an exercise in discernment and/or wisdom. However, the very act of judging will in and of itself cause a "yes/no" type of response. This will inevitably cause the formation of opposing groups, or simply two opposing people. Subsequently, any wisdom in a given situation will tend to be lost. The act of judging often has little or nothing to do with wisdom or discernment. In a society that is ostensibly merit-based,

_____

_____

_____

snap judgments or unfounded judgments are all too common. They can be divisive and we must take care not to let them become so.

Harmony in life or a relationship may only exist because those people who march to the beat of a different drum are simply silenced. The illusion of harmony can be powerful, particularly to an outside observer. This silencing in a relationship can have far-reaching and negative consequences. Some examples of silencing are belittling comments made to or about your partner (particularly in the presence of others), providing negative criticism for your partner's efforts, and failing to support your partner when he or she is being challenged by another person, to name a few. The silencing of one's partner (in a relationship) by the other can lead to insecurities, resentment, and the eventual breakdown of the relationship. Relationship breakdown is far from inevitable though, as it can be very difficult to leave an inharmonious situation. To an outside observer, however, a harmonious state may well still exist. For example, people looking in on a relationship may see a state which does not actually represent the true state of affairs. This misconception is a common occurrence.

As we examine our life, we may, among other things, be looking for authenticity. Living an authentic life requires us to examine our values — what we believe, having a sense of right and wrong, having a sense of good and bad, and remaining yourself, which can be difficult if you are in an abusive, silencing situation. We need to develop a sense of integrity. A sense of integrity relates to general character. Part of our sense of integrity is developing a formal relationship with ourselves and subsequently developing

---

---

a connection to moral behaviour. Once we are able to do this we can define and set boundaries. This will reinforce self-esteem and also promote our own emotional health.

In identifying our strengths and weaknesses we are able to improve ourselves. A sign of emotional maturity is the ability to recognise and accept our strengths and weaknesses and then move on so as to not be fettered by weaknesses or inflated by strengths. We can also address our limiting beliefs, such as unrealistic social, religious, and familial expectations, as these may hold us back by crowding us with false fears and doubts.

Another facet of authenticity is communication skills. Having a healthy and meaningful relationship (either personally or professionally) depends on these skills. If your communication skills are poor, then you may inadvertently push people away and thus limit opportunities for real connections to develop. When communicating, listen to what is said as well as what is not said. Be present in the moment: "I am here for you" is a powerful phrase. For David and Joanne it means: "You have my undivided attention and I will always do my best to understand and/or help you." As you communicate, remember to spend time listening, *really* listening. True listening will foster completeness. Keep your communication honest, open, and two-way. Just as it isn't what you see but how you see it that matters, it isn't what you hear, but how you listen. Make an effort to understand, even if you can't fully understand.

Depending on how we live, our emotions/feelings can either belong to us or we can belong to them. We need to pay careful attention to them in

_____

_____

_____

order to fully understand ourselves. Emotions can be situation-dependent. Ideally, we want to govern our emotions. The more in tune we are with ourselves, the easier this will be.

People's reactions to the happiness of others vary considerably. Why would you not want your partner to be happy? Why would you not spoil them? For example, Joanne's friends reacted with surprise to Joanne telling them that she gets up every morning with David and makes breakfast for both of them.

Do people fear making others happy? Why is there fear or shock at the thought of making others (your partner) happy? Perhaps the fear comes from putting in effort (trust) and it not being reciprocated. Could this fear be from unrealistic expectations of ourselves or of our partner?

Why do people look for faults/chinks/problems in the relationships of happy people? Because they are unsatisfied or unhappy and don't like the thought of others being happy if they are not. They may think of themselves as one of life's victims. For example, David and Joanne were asked why they weren't at home doing housework instead of enjoying all of the rich experiences life has to offer. It's possible to do both, yet some find it foreign that others have so much fun.

Schadenfreude

> *"Even when there is no tangible benefit to the observer or*
> *some social justice served, (other people's) misfortunes are*

_____

_____

_____

pleasurable in part because they make people feel better about themselves. It seems to be born out of social comparison process. If I compare myself with others, and find I am not as good (as they are), I am much more likely to be pleased when they are taken down a notch."

Mina Cikara, Harvard University

Schadenfreude has existed as long as humanity. Lucretius, a Roman poet and philosopher, said this while watching a fleet sail out into a storm:

"It is sweet to perceive from what misfortunes you yourself are free."

There is joy in a battle won or in seeing a rival cut down to size. Even if we won't admit it to ourselves, we get a certain pleasure from seeing these things. For example, we may feel pleasure when a politician is caught in the wrong. It may have nothing at all to do with jealousy on our part — we may simply be resentful of the importance we have ascribed them only to see them abuse their power and get caught. If we then see them punished, this can raise our own status, even if it is only in our minds! People can also enjoy vicarious sadness and misery. There are always those who love a good disaster as long as it is happening to someone else. We find it reassuring to hear about the misfortunes of others. Others' misfortunes remind us that it isn't only our own hopes and or dreams that don't work out — everyone else's are dashed too.

_____

_____

_____

SOMETHING TO CHEW ON....

1. What differences in the outcome/s of a situation have you noticed when you take responsibility for your actions rather than blaming someone else for them?

2. When is it less easy to be a positive person?

3. It's not what you see but how you look at it that matters. How often do you look at things and consider them from different perspectives?

4. Think of a time when you did not like the story you were in. Were you able to change your story? If so, what did it take to make the change? If not, why were you unable to do so?

5. How did you respond to a time in your past when you were silenced? Would you respond the same way now?

6. In what situations have you exercised schadenfreude? What were your motivations for doing so?

_____

_____

_____

SOMETIMES WE MUST CARRY THE YAK

As told by Holt the Yak...

Fate gives us that one person
Who bestows light
On the tall shadows
That extend down through time
And continue to mark us today.
tpb

The day of the yak came after a time of difficulty and uncertainty from not knowing when or where they would see each other again. They had been living two separate lives while continuing to grow together and support each other. It was at this point when David and Joanne came to know and believe that they were there for each other, and they would carry each other whenever needed.

Each day we may be surrounded by angels in different disguises. They can be our inner voice or external callings. If they are our inner voice, do we make the effort to listen deeply? Do we act on what we hear? Is the wisdom of which we are capable utilized at all? External callings can come from different sources. They can come from people, places, jobs, etc. Do we feel more susceptible to external callings because we feel pressured by them? For example, we may feel pressured by the distracting influence of delegated tasks at work, or perhaps your child having a tantrum when you are out somewhere. Generally, these external pressures demand considerable attention. Failure to deal with these pressures may cause health deterioration or leaving a job. In leaving a job, that particular calling is decisively removed. Being guided by your heart will enable you to focus more fully on your internal callings and allow you to grow as a person. Our internal callings can be easy to ignore as the only person who will ever judge them is ourselves. However, there are times when we ignore these callings at our peril. It can be difficult to know if they are calling us and if they are, is there a right way or a wrong way to go? There is always a way to go. We make the choice, choose our direction, and off we go. The way could be right, wrong, or neutral. Depending on the path you choose (or happen to be stuck on), you may need to stay at a job so as to pay your bills, or you may even need to stay with a partner for the same reason. Sometimes we stay in an undesirable situation because we hope it will get better. Often, it does not. Sometimes we simply need to have the courage to simply go. We can then (as we move) evaluate our decisions. If there does not appear to be a right or wrong way, we may simply be guided by our heart to those

_____

_____

_____

appointments that life has put there for us to keep. If it appears that there is no particular way that is beckoning us, then we may indeed be guided by our hearts. Sometimes we go alone to these appointments, sometimes we take someone to help us, and sometimes we help another.

There is considerable risk in following your heart to these appointments. There are always sacrifices to be made when following your heart. However, if you are indeed following your true heart, you will be going the right way. Further to this, if you firmly believe following your heart is the right way, it will not necessarily be easier, but it may give you more comfort (knowing that your choice is right). If, however, you are confident and approach the appointments with an open heart, then you can meet these uncertainties or help others to meet them. This in turn can lead to a very real and authentic future that you have chosen for yourself rather than one you have settled for — not an easy task! A life chosen is a life in which you have followed your heart. It is a terrible feeling to settle for a life when you believe you do not have a choice. Do we always allow ourselves to have choices? This can lead to difficulty in looking at the truth — we don't want to believe we are settling for a life, even though we may be afraid of the risks associated with choosing our lives. For example, you may remain in a long-term relationship because you believe it's the right thing to do, even though you may feel as if you are drowning. When you really want a relationship to be right, and it just isn't, this is when your heart will suffer.

In a relationship we often say that two people join together to become one. This is true in many instances. For example, when identifying a problem,

_____

_____

_____

two people can join together to solve the difficulty. Also, when enjoying an experience together, two people become one, perhaps sharing the dance.

However, there are times when the two who have joined together to become one must part temporarily and become two again. This may happen in order to achieve a personal goal, complete a job, or help a family member. These two things happen normally throughout a healthy, loving, and supportive relationship.

On the other hand, there may be periods of time when one individual in a relationship must carry out the tasks of both partners. In this case, one individual becomes two. If this is a temporary situation, due to an illness, work, or personal difficulties, it can cause a relationship to become stronger. This is carrying the yak. However, if this situation is prolonged, perhaps due to lack of support, then this can become damaging to a relationship. The individual who is taking the role of two may lose their authenticity or simply give up. This then becomes a one-sided relationship. This is not the same as carrying the yak.

Our inner self consists of the way in which our environment responds to us. If our inner sense of being becomes lost, we may become inwardly divided. Our outer sense of self is how we respond to our environment. If our outer sense of being becomes lost, we may lose track of where we are or where we need to go. If you are inwardly divided in a relationship, your partner may not know how to respond to you. In turn, you may not know how to respond to them. If communication is not practiced (for example, "I am here for you; what do you need?", "I need help"), then the

_____

_____

_____

relationship can be on very shaky ground. If we are able to realise that we are lost (either on our own or with the help and guidance of another) and we can accept this, being lost can lead us to the place we need to be in order to find or heal ourselves. From this point on we can be fully engaged in life. As we move through life, we need to respond to all of the experiences and events that we seek out or encounter. It would behoove us to move through and respond to these experiences. If, as may happen, your heart is breaking, your inner turmoil is too great, or you have nothing left to give, there comes a time when you need to make a decision that will change your circumstances. It can, at times, be difficult to do this, but with the help of a supportive and loving partner we can face the challenges that arise, move past them, and continue to grow.

Difficulties and challenges that are before us may be obstacles that occur randomly or deliberately. They may be put there in our path so as to exploit our weaknesses or impede our progress. It may take an outside observer to help us to determine which of these two possibilities are occurring at any given time. By recognising what is happening, either alone or with help, we can move on through these experiences and they will form part of the perpetually ongoing emergence of who we are. Part of our being is made up of past events and these will help to shape us. If we so choose, we can learn and grow from these experiences.

Life's plans for us rarely coincide with our plans for life! They may in fact be at considerable variance. In order for us to ride along on the waves of life's plan (instead of being swamped by it), then we must be flexible,

---

---

adaptable, and willing to change. Apparently simple plans or expectations may require considerable complexity if they are to be realised. As a result, we may well require the assistance of others.

The path is there for us to take advantage of, to strive to maintain, and also to take joy from and delight in. It is the path itself that guides you, providing you stay on the path and read the signs that it presents along the way. These signs can, of course, be misread — they may not be for you or they could provide a detour along the way. Your path is a journey made of three parts: a journey (where you have to go), a newness (where you are in the present moment), and a distance covered (where you have already been). An individual's path consists of all of these elements and the signs along the way will tell you where you are, where you have been (although we are considerably more than simply the sum of our past), where you are going, and where you need to go.

Where you are going and where you need to be may be completely different places. Everywhere we go and everything we do is for a reason, even though that reason may not be readily apparent at any given moment in the present.

As you travel along your path, be better than you were before. Take advantage of what your path offers you and how present opportunities enable you to conquer the next obstacle. The next obstacle may be self-imposed or from an external influence. In following a particular course of action, the freedom is always there to decide what to do, although we don't always see it. Options may not always be seen, but they are present.

Your path in life can actually be your goal. Your particular path is unlike any other and comprises the way you live, act, think, and feel. It is uniquely yours alone. However, we are never alone on this path. Others have been on it before us, some are on this path with us now, and more will also be there in the future. Even though we may not know who these others are, we can take comfort in the knowledge that they are nonetheless real and present. These others could be anybody or someone significant to us. For example, we may be following the same path that an unknown grandparent trod before us, or we may be moving along the path together with a loved one.

Your life will bring many experiences and you must learn to pick and choose from among them. Those experiences that are detracting from your life should be dismissed and those that are nurturing you and helping you to grow should be fostered. Accept what your path has to offer and learn the lessons it provides. Face these considerable challenges that we all face. Many people are not able to face these challenges alone. If you have such problems when it comes to learning life's lessons, then you will, in all probability, find yourself confronted with situations in which you are forced to deal with the repercussions of these lessons. You need to learn from these lessons and move on so you will not be bound to keep repeating the same mistakes. Mistakes may not be recognised as lessons as they can come in many different forms.

Windows of opportunity may present themselves. They may only appear once in any particular form. If we fail to take advantage of these opportunities, then our life experiences can be the poorer for that inaction. It

_____

_____

_____

may also be difficult to recognise a window of opportunity as such and this can also hinder our ability to act on what is presented to us. For example, when David and Joanne were planning to run self-defence classes, they were looking for a padded suit for training. David mentioned this to one of his coworkers who informed him there was one available in stores. They purchased the suit and away they went. Had they failed to seize that simple opportunity, the classes would not have been the success they became. We can also create our own windows of opportunity, such as when David decided to join the army. This turned into a great series of experiences he could not have had anywhere else.

As long as you maintain a curiosity to see what is around the next turn and learn from these lessons, you will be able to keep moving along your path. A sense of wonder can help you to keep moving along the path – be it a well-worn one or the path not taken.

The Road Not Taken by Robert Frost

Two roads diverged in a yellow wood.
And sorry I could not travel both
And be one traveller, long I stood
And looked down one as far as I could
To where it bent in the undergrowth.

Then took the other, as just as fair,
And having perhaps the better claim,
Because it was grassy and wanted wear;

———————————————————————

———————————————————————

———————————————————————

Though as for the passing there
Had worn them really about the same,

And had that morning equally lay
In leaves no step had trodden black.
Oh, I kept the first for another day!
Yet knowing how way leads onto way,
I doubted if I should ever come back.

I shall be telling this with a sigh
Somewhere ages and ages hence:
Two roads diverged in a wood, and I-

I took the one less travelled by,
And that has made all the difference.

Published in 1916 as the first poem in the Mountain Interval collection.

Part of any journey will cause fatigue at some point. Mental tiredness, however, is absolutely not the same as physical tiredness and should not be confused with it. Mental tiredness can often be relieved by exercise. Mental tiredness is more draining than physical tiredness; it feeds on itself and can become a self-perpetuating monster — it can be very difficult for one to see in oneself and may require outside assistance to acknowledge and overcome. This tiredness can also cause an embargo response. This is a common response to fear, sorrow, or depression. It involves the presence of distractors — TV, music, magazines, alcohol, etc. Using these distractions only helps us to move away from our self. Even though you

_____

_____

_____

can't always see it, there is always blue sky above the clouds, and it may take the help and support of another for us to realise this.

Our memories can cause us real and genuine suffering. This suffering can be both mental and physical, even though the memories are not occurring in the present moment. If we are able to recognise that we are in the habit of replaying past events, for example, replaying certain types of trauma in our past, and if we react to these events as if they were currently occurring, then we can remind ourselves (or be reminded) that there is another route we can take. We can look at and live in the moment as it exists right now and leave the past for another time when we are able to examine it with compassion. The present moment is where we need to be functioning.

"Let the fear come up and fall though the other side."

From the Wisdom Way of Knowing
by Cynthia Bourgeault

———————————————————————————————

———————————————————————————————

———————————————————————————————

SOMETHING TO CHEW ON...

1. What form do your life's appointments take?

   For example: -advantageous

                           -hazardous

                           -neither

   How do they differ with the presence of another?

2. What does your dance look like?

3. Do your inner and outer selves mirror and reflect each other?

4. Would you say that you are living your life as a journey or as a goal?

5. Think about what an embargo response means to you. Think of a time when you were overtaken by embargo responses. What were the outcomes?

_____

_____

_____

LOVE IN THE HOT SPRINGS – AND THE CORKS BOBBED BY

As told by Holt the Yak...

And their souls waltzed across the universe
tpb

To be compatible in loving another in the most unconditional way possible first requires knowledge and love of oneself.

> *"I came to the conclusion that the most important thing in life is not achievement, but that humble, yet difficult - ability to remain myself."*
>
> *Svetlana Alliluyeva*

How do we develop this knowledge and love? The process will of course be different for everyone. For example, growing up in an abusive household tends to cause self-love to not happen, whereas self-love is far more likely to occur in a warm and loving household. The way in which self-love occurs will vary depending on the personal situation of each individual. We may have to work diligently to foster this love of self. The outcome of this diligence can set the conditions for loving another. Our relationship with our self, others, and our environment affect how profoundly and unconditionally we can love others. How we react to our environment and how it reacts to us can allow us to function well. For example, spending time with like-minded people can be far more constructive in cultivating personal growth.

By spending time in the company of toxic people, the reverse outcome is likely, which causes us to shut down in order to distance ourselves from the situation we are in. It is part of the relationship that we need to master in order to move forward both with our relationship with self and relationships with others. We need to beware of becoming used to an environment surrounded by toxic people. If you become comfortable with this type of situation, when you are eventually able to leave it, you may well walk right back into another similar situation.

We cannot trust others to love us until we love ourselves. When we choose to trust others to love us, we can genuinely be there in the present moment for them. At this point of trust, we can journey forward together. We know we are at this point when we are aware of the fact that we don't only have ourselves.

———————————————————————————————

———————————————————————————————

———————————————————————————————

*"I know that no matter what happens you will not stop loving
me, because you trust me to love you under any conditions
and it is reciprocated. I will not do anything to intentionally
harm you. I feel safe with you, I love you, and I trust
you unconditionally."*

Joanne Mytts

In the context of this quotation, "feeling safe" refers to being loved unconditionally without judgment or fear of being cast aside.

Love is born on the grounds of understanding, an understanding which is able to help us to allay our doubts or our fears. With love at first sight, a look or gaze is caught between two people. As the gaze is caught, something passes between. It may be felt as energy or it may be felt as vibrations. It moves in both directions and is therefore a conscious act on the part of the two people. We can perceive it moving in both directions when giving and receiving tend to merge to become one thing, moving in a constant cyclic pattern. Because it is a conscious act, it can give us a forward direction and ultimately become the path along which we shall travel together.

SOMETHING TO CHEW ON....

1. Think of a time when you have been both immersed and enveloped in a moment. Nobody affected you and you affected nobody. These moments only happen once and then time and space move on. Do these moments create themselves, or do you create these moments?

_____

_____

_____

SO, HERE ARE THE REFERENCES I USED...

Bourgeault, C. (2003). *The wisdom way of knowing.* San Francisco, CA: Wiley and Sons.

Bourgeault, C. (2005). *The meaning of Mary Magdalene.* Boston, MA: Shambala Publications.

Cikara, M., et al. (2014). Their pain gives us pleasure: How intergroup dynamics shape empathetic failures and counter empathetic responses. *Social Psychology, 55,* p. 110-125.

Csikszentmihalyi, M. (1996). *Creativity: Flow and the psychology of discovery and invention.* New York, NY: Harper Perennial.

Csikszentmihalyi, M., & Csikzsentmihalyi, I. S. (Eds.). (1998). *Optimal experience: Psychological studies of flow in consciousness.* Cambridge, United Kingdom: Cambridge University Press.

Descartes, R. (1985). *The passions of the soul in the philosophical writings of Descartes* (Vol. 1). (J. Cottingham et al., Trans.). Cambridge, United Kingdom: Cambridge University Press.

Festinger, L. (1962). *A theory of cognitive dissonance*. Stanford, CA: Stanford University Press.

Frost, R. (1916). *Mountain interval*. Jefferson, NC: Henry Holt.

King, K. (2003). *The Gospel of Mary*. Santa Rosa, CA: Polebridge Press.

Merton, T. (2005). *No man is an island*. Boston, MA: Shambhala.

Merton, T. (2007). *New seeds of contemplation*. New York, NY: New Directions Publishing Corporation.

Meyer, M., & Robinson, J. M. (2007). *The Nag Hammadi scriptures: The international edition*. New York, NY: Harper Collins.

Oxford dictionary of physics. (2009). London, United Kingdom: Oxford University Press.

Rilke, R. M. (1984). *Letters to a young poet*. (S. Mitchell, Trans.). New York, NY: Random House.

Sartre, J.-P. (2007). *Existentialism*. Retrieved from http://www.iep.edu/sartre-ex/,

Sartre, J.-P. (2015). *Existentialism and human emotions*. Retrieved from http://www.philosophymagazine.com/others/MO_Sartre_Existentialism.html

Starbird, M. (1993). *The woman with the alabaster jar*. Rochester, VT: Bear and Company.

_____

_____

_____

Thich, N. H. (2009). *You are here*. Boulder, CO: Shambala Publications.

Welwood, J. (1979). Psychology, science, and spiritual paths: Contemporary issues with Karl Pribram, Fritjof Capra, Huston Smith, Jacob Needleman, Roger Walsh, and Marilyn Ferguson. *Journal of Transpersonal Psychology, 10*(2), p. 93-111.

Welwood, J. (2003). *Double vision duality and nonduality in human experience*. Retrieved from http://www.johnwelwood.com/articles/DoubleVision.pdf

Welwood, J. (2005). *Intimate relationship as a spiritual crucible*. Retrieved from http://www.johnwelwood.com/articles/Relationship_as_a_Spiritual_Crucible_website.pdf

Wittgenstein, L. (1980). *Culture and value*. (P. Winch, Trans.). Chicago, IL: University of Chicago Press.

Well, that's that for now. Off to convalesce and wait until it's warm enough to get my bike out of hibernation and get on with the next book... *The Steel Yak*.

CPSIA information can be obtained
at www.ICGtesting.com
Printed in the USA
LVHW03s0003140918
589985LV00001B/60/P

9 780228 800361